Weight is the measurement of how heavy something is. Volume is how much space something takes up.

Volume

We usually measure volume in **millilitres (ml)** and **litres (l)**.

- There are **1,000ml** in **1l**.

- **1ml** is like a raindrop.

- **1l** is like a bottle of squash.

When you **measure** things in a beaker like this, make sure your eye is level with the level of the liquid when you read the scale.

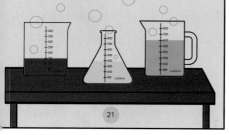

21

4 Try using these maths facts in your everyday life.

Written by David Kremer
Illustrated by Ian Cunliffe

Published by Ladybird Books Ltd
A Penguin Company
Penguin Books Ltd, 80 Strand, London WC2R 0RL, UK
Penguin Books Australia Ltd, Camberwell, Victoria, Australia
Penguin Books (NZ) Ltd, Private Bag, 102902, NSMC, Auckland 10, New Zealand

1 3 5 7 9 10 8 6 4 2

© LADYBIRD BOOKS MMV

ISBN-13: 978-1-84422-624-5
ISBN-10: 1-84422-624-7

Printed in China

Maths for School

Shapes

This is a **square**. It has four sides, all the same length.

This is a **rectangle**. It has two short sides and two longer sides.

This is a **triangle**. It has three sides but they are NOT always the same length.

This is a **circle**. How many sides does this have?

Every **shape** has features or properties such as number of sides or types of corners that make it different from other shapes.

Practise spotting these shapes whilst on car journeys!

This is a **cuboid**. It has six sides (also called **surfaces**) and eight corners (also called **vertices**). It has 12 edges. A cube is a special cuboid in which the edges are all the same length.

This is a **sphere**. It is a perfect ball shape.

This is a **cone**. It has two surfaces. One is a flat circle, and the other is curved up to the point.

This is a **cylinder**. It has three surfaces, a circle at each end and a third curved surface joining the edges of the two circles.

7

Patterns and sequences

A **pattern** is a series of repeated shapes, colours or numbers. This is a **colour pattern**:

The rule is ● ○ ● (red, yellow, blue) and then repeat...

This is a **shape** pattern:

The rule is circle, square, rectangle and then repeat...

This is a pattern of **colour** AND **shape**:

In a sequence, all the numbers may be different but they all have something in common.

A sequence is a line of shapes, colours or numbers arranged in order.

This is a number sequence:

2 4 6 8 10 12 14

The rule is to **add 2** to the previous number.

This is a different number sequence:

17 14 11 8 5 2

The rule is **take away 3** from the previous number.

Patterns and sequences have rules. You need to work out the rule to continue the sequence.

Size and order

To sort objects you need to decide on a type of measurement (called **criteria**) for example **weight**, **size** or **value**.

These coins are in **value** order but NOT in **size** order!

These planks of wood are sorted and arranged in order of **width**:

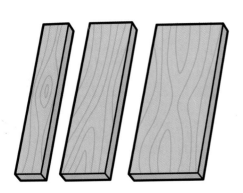

When you put things in a particular order you must first decide what rules to use: height, weight, amount, etc.

These vessels are arranged in order of **how much water** they can hold:

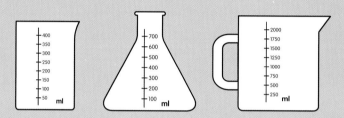

These melons are lined up in order of **size**:

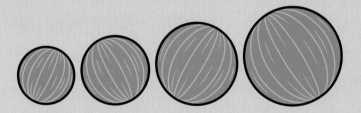

Some different **criteria**:

length   height   softness

brightness   alphabetical order

Partitioning

Numbers can be **split up** like the example below.

| 123 | is the same as | 100 | + 20 | + 3 |

This is called **partitioning**.

Here is another way of showing how to partition a number.

hundreds	tens	units
1	2	3

Here are some numbers already partitioned. Can you say what they are?

H	T	U
	4	6
3	5	9

How would you partition the number 945?

Partitioning a number into hundreds, tens and units is called 'place value'.

What about a number with a **0** in? Look at these numbers.

305

In this number there is nothing in the '**tens**' column.

350

In this number there is nothing in the '**units**' column.

So we have to use **0** as a '**place-holder**'. If we took the **0** away then both of these numbers would look the same.

Can you **partition** these numbers?

10	200
333	24
945	610

Draw a chart showing hundreds, tens and units and put each number in the right column.

Addition and subtraction

Addition

If you see these words in a maths problem, it means that you have to do an addition sum.

4 **plus** 4
4 **add** 4
4 **and** 4 make 8
4 **more than** 4 is 8

When you need to add larger numbers, or several numbers at once, a good way to do it is to partition the number and add the hundreds, tens and then the units.

For example: 47 + 22

can be worked out like this:

40	+ 20	=	**60**
7	+ 2	=	**9**
60	+ 9	=	**69**

Subtraction

If you see these words in a maths problem it means that you have to do a subtraction sum.

15 **minus** 10 is 5

15 **take away** 10 is 5

10 **less than** 15 is 5

Find the difference between 10 and 5

You have 5. **How many more** to make 15?

You can find a small difference between two numbers by counting up from the lower number. For example: 42 - 39

Count up from 39 until you reach 42.

The answer is 3.

15

Multiplying and dividing

If you see the following words it means that you must do a **multiplication** sum.

Find the **product** of 3 and 2.

What is 3 **times** 2?

What are **three twos**?

What are 3 **lots of** 2?

What is 3 **multiplied by** 2?

Multiplying is a quick way to add up:

Count the squares of chocolate.

We could count the squares like this:
3 + 3 + 3 + 3 + 3 = 15

Another way to write this is:

5 x 3 = 15

If you see these words it means that you must do a **division** sum.

> **Divide** 10 between 5 people.
> **Share** 10 between 5 baskets.
> What is 10 **divided by** 5?

Division is similar to **sharing**.

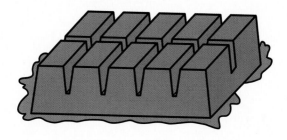

If you wanted to divide this bar of chocolate between 5 people, you could do it like this:

10 **shared** 5 ways = 2 or 10 **divided by** 5 = 2

Each person would get 2 squares of chocolate.

Another way to write this is:

$$10 \div 5 = 2$$

Measuring length

We usually measure length in **millimetres** (**mm**), **centimetres** (**cm**), **metres** (**m**), and **kilometres** (**km**).

10mm = **1cm**

100cm = **1m**

1,000m = **1km**

It is very important to use the correct type of **length measurement** for the thing that you are measuring.

Finding the length of an ant = **millimetres**

Building a wall = **centimetres**

Marking a running track = **metres**

Going on a journey = **kilometres**

Length is how we know how long something is, or how far away a place is.

As well as deciding what units, (**mm**, **cm** or **m**) you will use, you must decide what tool you are going to use to measure. Here are some different types.

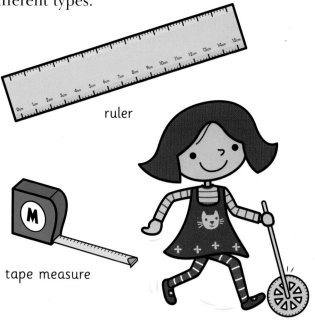

ruler

tape measure

trundlewheel

Whatever **distance** you are measuring you must always be certain that your ruler, tape or trundlewheel starts on **0**.

Measuring

Weight

We usually measure weight in **grams (g)** and **kilograms (kg)**.

- There are **1,000g** in **1kg.**

- **1g** is roughly the weight of a feather.

- **1kg** is roughly the weight of a large bag of flour.

When you **weigh** things you use scales. Always make sure that the dial says **0** before you place anything onto the scales.

Can you read these **weights**?

Weight is the measurement of how heavy something is.
Volume is how much space something takes up.

Volume

We usually measure volume in **millilitres (ml)** and **litres (l)**.

- There are **1,000ml** in **1l.**

- **1ml** is like a raindrop.

- **1l** is like a bottle of squash.

When you **measure** things in a beaker like this, make sure your eye is level with the level of the liquid when you read the scale.

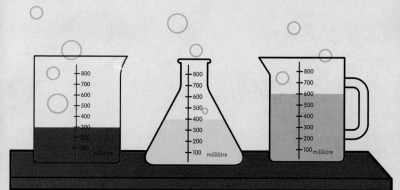

Can you read these **volumes**?

Time

The hands on a clock always go round in the same direction – **clockwise**.

cuckoo
cuckoo
cuckoo

The short hand tells the **hour**. There are 24 hours in a day, so the short hand must go round the whole clock face twice.

The long hand tells the **minutes**. There are 60 minutes in 1 hour so each number is worth 5 minutes. This hand goes all the way round the clock face in the time it takes the short hand to go from one number to the next.

When the minute hand points to 3, 6, 9 or 12
we use particular words to say what the time is.
Look at the examples below.

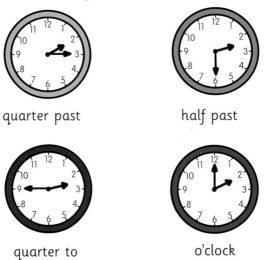

quarter past   half past

quarter to   o'clock

When the long hand is on the right, the minutes
are '**past the hour**'.

When the long hand is on the left, the minutes are
'**to the hour**'.

23

Symmetry

A shape has **symmetry** if you can fold it perfectly.

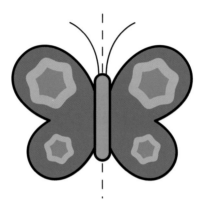

A butterfly is a good example. The wings are the same size, shape and have the same colouring. They fold on top of each other perfectly.

A shape can have more than one line of symmetry. For example, a square has four.

Folding is the same as **reflecting** in a mirror. If you put a mirror on a shape and it reflects back the same image then it must be **symmetrical**.

The fold or mirror line that produces a perfect reflection is also called the **'line of symmetry'**.

An image is **symmetrical** to its reflection.

Money

Money comes in **coins**

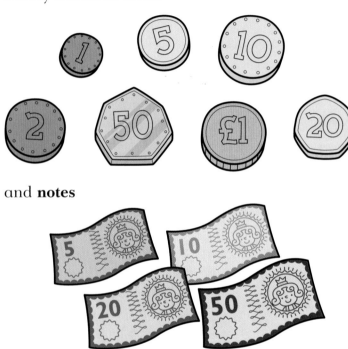

and **notes**

There are **100** pennies in **£1**, **1000** pennies in **£10** and **10,000** pennies in **£100**.

There are lots of different ways to make up an amount of money. These sets of coins, for example, are all different ways to make 50p.

(50) = 50p

(20) (20) (10) = 50p

(20) (10) (10) (5) (1) (1) (1) (1) (1) = 50p

(20) (10) (5) (5) (5) (2) (2) (1) = 50p

Change is what you get back from a shopkeeper when you don't have the exact money to pay for something.

If you gave £1 for this bag of sweets then you need to take away 60p (what it costs) from 100p (what you gave).

100 - 60 = 40

So you should get 40p change.

Pictograms

Pictograms are useful drawings or charts to help you compare **amounts**.

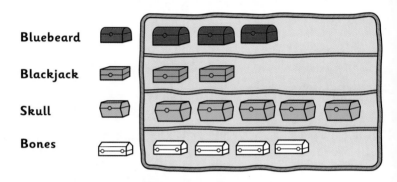

It is easy to see from the pictogram that Captain Skull has the **most** treasure and Captain Blackjack has the **least**!

Pictures help us to compare numbers and amounts quickly and easily.

Sometimes each picture counts as a certain **number**. In this case, we could say that each crossbones picture counts as **£100.**

Blackjack   Skull   Bones

So Captain Skull has:

5 x £100 or £500

whilst poor Captain Blackjack only has:

2 x £100 or £200

Quick facts

Words that mean +

plus
2 and 2 make
more than
add

Words that mean −

minus
take away
less than
find the difference
how many more

Words that mean x

times
lots of
what are three twos
multiplied by

Words that mean ÷

divide
share
divided by